30 DAYS TO YOUR DREAMS

DR. HENRY CLOUD

Published by
THOMAS NELSON
Since 1798

www.thomasnelson.com

30 Days to Your Dreams

© 2007 by Henry Cloud

Published in Nashville, TN by Thomas Nelson, Inc.

Cover Design: Linda Bourdeaux
Interior Design: Rainbow Graphics

ISBN-10: 0-7852-2780-6
ISBN-13: 978-7-8522-7806-1

Printed in the United States of America
07 08 09 10 11 RRD 9 8 7 6 5 4 3 2 1

DEDICATION

This book is dedicated to all those people who want to take a step of faith, dig up that talent, and make it a reality. God bless you!

CONTENTS

Acknowledgments vii

Opening Story: Finding Eden 1

PART I: THE CONTEXT

Day 1   Acknowledge the Source 8

Day 2   See Yourself as God Does 13

Day 3   Uncover Your Dreams 20

Day 4   Identify Your Relationship Dreams 25

Day 5   Distinguish between Dreams
and Fantasies 30

PART II: FIGURE OUT YOUR DREAM

Day 6   Act in Line with Your Abilities 36

Day 7   Unearth the Talent Buried in the Ground . . . 41

Day 8   Play the Movie 44

Day 9   Get Specific about Your Dream 50

Day 10   Lay One Brick at a Time 54

PART III: PLAN AHEAD

Day 11   Create a Plan 60

Day 12   Plan the Critical Path 64

Day 13   Determine What Has to Go 67

Day 14   Get Resources 71

Day 15   Seek Wisdom and Knowledge 74

PART IV: PROTECT YOUR DREAM

Day 16   Anticipate Obstacles 78

Day 17   Assemble Your Team 81

Day 18   Force Accountability 85

Day 19   Steer Clear of Unsafe People 89

Day 20   Quarantine Your Weaknesses 93

PART V: IMPLEMENT YOUR DREAM

Day 21   Monitor External Forces 98

Day 22   Get Comfortable with Process 101

Day 23   Evaluate Your Progress and Your Heart 106

Day 24   Conduct a Spiritual Checkup 109

Day 25   Reward Yourself 115

PART VI: MOVE FORWARD

Day 26   Take Time for a Reality Check 118

Day 27   Enjoy an Inspiration Day 122

Day 28   Notice Your Triggers 124

Day 29   Assess Your Progress and Plan
          for the Future 126

Day 30   Recommit for the Future 129

ACKNOWLEDGMENTS

I would like to acknowledge and thank the following people for making this workbook possible:

To Mary Graham for talking me into writing anything in the first place! Many years ago, you pushed me to write down my ideas, and now after all these years, you are pushing me to write this one. Thanks for your invitation to join Women of Faith, and for your commitment to people's growth.

To Shannon Miser-Marven for shepherding the whole project from the beginning. You nurtured the concept of "Token Male" for Women of Faith and brought everyone together, and then made the workbook a reality.

To Sheila Walsh, my old pal, for welcoming me into the fold and partnering in the Dreams conference. It is always fun to work with you.

OPENING STORY

ᴼᴼ Finding Eden ᴼᴼ

Imagine that one day you went out for a walk, and an angel came up to you and said, "Would you please come with me for a while?"

"What?" you reply. "Who are you? Where are we going? Why do you want to take *me*?"

"Don't worry," the angel says. "I promise it will be nice. I'm taking you to a place where all your dreams come true. Whatever you desire will become a reality. All you have to do is come with me—and trust me."

Would you go? Why or why not? Would you believe there is such a place? Would you believe the angel is real? Would you dare to believe that your dreams could come true? Would you think that he got the wrong person? Or would you think that dreams come true just in fairy tales?

Well, I'm no angel, but I am going to ask you to do something very similar to what that angel did in our hypothetical situation. I am going to ask you to go on a journey with me for thirty days to find, or rediscover, your own dreams for your life and then to make them come true. Impossible? Before you dismiss the idea, consider this: You were designed for just such a place and just such a life. Really. That is not a Disney fairy tale. That is ultimate reality. The problem is that many of us have forgotten that it is ultimate reality. We live in a false reality, one where we have lost the ability to dream and to believe that dreams come true. We live in an upside-down world, as it were. In the real world—the world God created—you were made to dream and to fulfill those dreams. That was God's plan. And that is no fairy tale. That was the original plan for you and me on planet Earth.

God made us to be like him. We were created in his image to do what he does. We were supposed to think of what we wanted and then use our hearts, minds, souls, and strength to make that happen . . . just like he does. God dreams up things based on his desires, and then he brings them to fruition. In fact, his desires *are* his will. In the original Hebrew language these words are often interchangeable. There is no difference between God's desire and what he wills to happen. He dreams; therefore, it is.

We were to be like that too. Not that we could be God, dreaming up new universes and then—*poof!*—there they would be. But we were designed to desire things and then bring them into being. That is a big part of what it means to be human. We can dream, and then bring those dreams about. That's no pie-in-the-sky New Age thought. That is the real world as God created it.

So what were we intended to dream of and create? First, good and fulfilling relationships and, second, a meaningful expression of our gifts and talents. We were made to be connected to God and other people in deep and significant ways, and we were made to take our gifts and talents into the world and accomplish things with them that fulfill us and help others. God put Adam and Eve in the garden to enjoy him, each other, and all of his creation. He told them to rule and subdue the earth—to use their brains, talents, and abilities *and* to have a good time. The world was their oyster, and they had all that they needed to make it all happen.

THE BIG DISCONNECT

That's the life that you were created to have. So, why isn't it happening for you? Well, the Bible explains that too. It says that we lost it. We decided that being human—with all of that great potential and giftedness—was not enough. We wanted more. We wanted to be God. So we gave up our humanity and all of our abilities to dream and to make those dreams happen. When we moved away from God, the whole divine arrangement turned upside down. Some terrible things happened that are still affecting us today.

First, we lost our connection to God. We lost the relationship that gave us life as well as all of our abilities and all of our resources. It was as if we unplugged from the Source of all that we needed to make the life we desire come true.

And when we did that, we lost our connection with one another. We covered up our real selves with a fig leaf and hid in our shame. Psychologists tell us all the time that we have lost our ability to be intimate with one another because of fears and hurts; we hide from one another in a prison of shame. We feel that we aren't good enough to really be loved, so we are no longer real with one another. As a result, we don't have the relationships we desire, nor are we able to help each other discover our dreams. Some of our deepest desires for love and accomplishment remain secret, lost in our hearts and souls. We fear that if we share them with others, we'll be criticized or further shamed. So we remain behind the fig leaf.

Thus, we have even lost our connection with ourselves. Our shame and fear have not only isolated us from God and one another. Our shame and fear have buried our own hearts and souls. We don't know our true dreams; they've been lost in hurt, fear, and distraction until our lives are devoid of true desire and, as a result, of true fulfillment.

That is where we usually live. Not everyone experiences this lostness to the same degree, but we all experience it to some degree. We have lost touch with God, the source of what we need to bring our dreams to fruition. We have lost touch with one another, the relationships that could help us fulfill our dreams. And we have lost touch with our own dreams. Anyone need an angel?

THE BIG RECONNECT

Fortunately, the story of the Bible doesn't end with our being lost. It says that God went looking for us. He saw us in our wandering, hiding, lost state and wanted to bring us back to the way things were supposed to be. He wanted to help us become the people he created us to be. Now, here's the fascinating part. That action on God's part is so *natural.* If you are a father and your son or daughter were lost, *naturally* you would go looking for that child and do whatever you could to help. Any father with a heart would say, "Hey, come back. Let me help you. I know how to do this. Just give me a chance!" It is the most natural thing in the world for a father to look for his lost child and to help him or her to get back on track.

But, for some reason, we don't think of it that way. Instead of seeing God as someone who wants to help us get back on track and make our dreams come true, we look at him through the wrong lenses. We look through our own shame and lostness, and instead of seeing a father who wants to make it all better, we see a cop who wants to read us a list of our failings, or an angry judge who wants to sentence us to jail, or a school principal who wants to send us to detention for all of our screwups. We look at him and think, *Oh, no. He's mad. Look at how I've messed up. I better hide even more. He's the last person I want to talk to!* So, we run even further away from the angry God who is going to make us feel even worse than we already do.

And here is where the angel comes in—and not as a cop or an angry judge, but as a father who comes to look for you and take you back to the way it was supposed to be. God came to earth looking for you. He wasn't mad, nor was he condemning. He even said, "I did not come to judge the world" (see John 12:47). Instead he said, "[I] came to seek and to save what was lost" (see Luke 19:10). God is literally looking for you and your lost ability to dream. He is the angel I asked you about in the beginning. He is the one who says, "Would you like to come with me to a place where you can dream again, a place where dreams come true?"

If that is your desire, then he can bring it about. In fact, it is why he came. God wants to restore you to the person he created you to be: a person connected to God, the Source of all things good; a person connected to others in fulfilling ways; and a person in touch with dreams and desires and able to become all he means you to be. For the next thirty days, we are going to take a look at how this story has played itself out in your life as well as how God can enter into your story and bring you back to Eden and to being the person you were meant to be.

THE JOURNEY BACK

In this workbook, we will look at three themes and how they are the key to rediscovering your dreams and making them a reality in your life:

- The you that you were created to be
- The things that have gone wrong that keep you from being that person
- God's plan to reconnect you to his original design for you

In this journey, we will take one day at a time, one principle at a time, and you will both rediscover the dreams that you have lost and find a path for bringing them to fruition. You will notice these three themes woven throughout the entire thirty days.

So, if you are ready for this journey to your own promised land, your own Eden, then all you have to do is be open. And if you can't be open, then at least be open to being open. God will do the rest. Remember, it was his original plan for you to have dreams and make them happen. And when those dreams were lost, it was he who came looking for you in order to restore that ability to dream and fulfill those dreams. He is definitely on your side.

As you go through these thirty days, you will find a new principle or practice each day that will not only serve you well for that day but will also be a building block for the days and months to come. Keep in mind that the process of reconnecting with God does not end with this book. These thirty days are just the beginning of a journey you will want to continue until seeing and pursuing your dreams has become an ongoing reality, a way of life, for you.

PART ONE:

~~§ The Context §~~

DAY 1

Acknowledge the Source

I don't know where you are coming from or what experiences you bring to this journey. You may have reached many goals and dreams, or you may have suffered discouragement time and again. You may have a lot of faith, or you may have very little. Whatever your past experience, I want you to begin on day one with a fresh start and one basic question: *What is your view of God when you think about reaching your dreams?*

Here are some possibilities:

- God isn't interested in my dreams or desires. He's only interested in my sacrifice and service. Dreams are selfish.

- God isn't even there. I prayed for his help before, and nothing happened, so why should I think that he is going to be there for me now?

- God doesn't really get involved in things like dreams and goals. He wants us to pursue them and to do it honestly and justly, but he leaves all of that up to us.

- God doesn't get involved, even if he exists. He just created things and lets them run their course. Life is really more about luck and our own effort.

- God has let so many bad things happen to me that there is no reason for me to think that he would do anything for me now.

Whatever your thoughts are, I am sure that you have come to those conclusions for reasons that make sense to you. But I want you to be open to seeing God from a different perspective. *I want you to be open to believing that God is interested in what you desire and that he actually will work with you to discover your dreams and bring them to fruition.*

God is the Source of all good things. No matter what bad things have happened to you in the past that wrecked your pursuit of dreams, God did not do that to you. It was probably people who did. Or, people taught you that God is not interested in your dreams, and so you have either given up on him as a source of help, or you are avoiding him because you don't see him as being on your side.

Here are some examples of what God says about you and your dreams:

> You [God] open your hand
> and satisfy the desires of every living thing.
> — PSALM 145:16

> He fulfills the desires of those who fear him;
> he hears their cry and saves them.
> — PSALM 145:19

> But seek first his kingdom and his righteousness,
> and all these things will be given to you as well.
> — MATTHEW 6:33

> Delight yourself in the LORD
> and he will give you the desires of your heart.
> — PSALM 37:4

As you probably know, God doesn't always protect us from other people hurting us. Nor is he a Santa Claus who gives us whatever we want. If at my height I dream, for example, of being an NBA basketball player, I can't think that God is going to make that happen. And I can't ask for life to be a place where I don't ever get hurt. But faith is about believing God despite all that confuses us about him. Faith in God is believing that he wants you to dream and to fulfill your dreams even when you have to sometimes grow into the *right* dream, as we shall see. Faith in God is believing that he still loves you and cares for you *even when others have hurt you and he did not stop them.* Jesus knows that experience very well, as do most people. But the reality is that God is bigger than this mixed-up life *and* bigger than our understanding of it. That is where faith and dreams intersect.

So I want you to take a step of faith and, no matter how it feels, to be open to seeing God as Someone who is going to partner with you in this process. The Bible says that God is the source of all good things, and I want you to *look to the Source and ask him to help you to both find your dreams and bring them into reality.* Today, Day 1, take these steps:

1. Surrender to God and ask him to help. In your own words—or using mine—pray something like this:

   Dear God, help me. I turn to you in faith, even with my doubts, and ask you to be the source of my dreams. Help me in this process to be healed of the things that have held me back. Help me to see who you created me to be. Show me the steps to take. Give me the strength and courage I will need. Guide me along the way.

Dear Jesus; Give me the faith and trust that You are the source of my dreams. Help me to see & to know who You created me to be & how to take those steps

Meditate on the verses above and then ask yourself the following questions:

2. Do you believe that God wants to fulfill your desires? Why or why not? What stands in the way of your believing that? What would need to happen for you to be able to believe this truth? Talk to God about your thoughts and feelings after reading those verses. Be honest with him. Tell him what you need.

Yes - Because He loves me and He created me to take the steps necessary to fulfill my dreams.

3. Call a friend and talk about those verses. Ask your friend to pray for you in this process, believing that God will help you pursue and fulfill your dreams.

4. Pick your favorite verse above or another one about God fulfilling your desires. Write it on an index card and paste it in a place you will see often.

5. Promise yourself that each day at a specific time you will ask God to lead you in this pursuit of your dreams.

Time ___:___ a.m./p.m.

Memory Verse

Trust in the LORD with all your heart
    and lean not on your own understanding;
in all your ways acknowledge him,
    and he will make your paths straight.
                    — PROVERBS 3:5–6

DAY 2

See Yourself as God Does

Yesterday we talked about who God is and how we can see him accurately. It is important to see that God really wants to help you uncover and realize your dreams and desires. So the next question becomes "Who is it that he wants to give these desires to?" In other words, who are *you*? Do you see yourself accurately? Do you see yourself as God sees you?

Your past experience may have taught you that you aren't important to anyone, that your desires and dreams don't matter. We know that children get their ideas about themselves not from a book or a philosophy, but from how they are treated. If their dreams and goals and their very selves are treated as important, then they will come to believe that they matter. But if children are ignored or criticized, they begin to ignore and criticize their own dreams as well. You might have come to believe that your dreams don't matter to anyone and that, just like you, they are not important.

So, if you are going to accomplish your dreams, it is important that you get a real view of yourself, to see yourself as God looks at you—and he sees you as very important to him. He takes pleasure in your well-being and fulfillment. In Psalm 35:27, he says it this way:

> May those who delight in my vindication
>   shout for joy and gladness;
> may they always say, "The LORD be exalted,
>   who *delights* in the well-being of his servant."
>   (emphasis added)

But, when it comes to your gifts and talents, God gets even more specific.

The Bible tells us that you are God's "workmanship." He created you for very specific reasons and purposes, and he wants you to go out and realize those things you have been created to do. Listen to how he says it:

> For we are God's workmanship, created in Christ
> Jesus to do good works, which God prepared in
> advance for us to do.
>   (EPHESIANS 2:10)

Now think about this. God has actually made you with certain gifts and abilities that are to be used to do good things. He constructed you to be who you are. He did that for a reason, for you to be fruitful and to do good things. So, when you have the desire to be fruitful and accomplish things, that is not just an idle wish God would want you to dismiss. The reality is exactly the opposite. God has an investment in you. It is as if he has bought an expensive piece of equipment to do a very specific job, and he naturally wants it to do that job. He wants you to be able to make that job happen. That's why he made you.

This truth is important because so many people want to be successful, but they think they're not the kind of people who become fruitful, the kind of people for whom life actually works. But you were created to be fruitful. As the saying goes, "God don't make no junk!" You were created by God to work, to be able to pull it off and make it happen! So start seeing yourself that way—and not as someone who wants to make it happen but can never pull it off. The Bible teaches that you were created and equipped to make it happen. There is no reason for you to think otherwise or for you to let other people or experiences define you.

I am not saying you *deserve* the life you always wanted. I don't believe we deserve a good life. Rather, I think that is the wrong issue to consider. Our life is not about what we deserve; it's about what God has done. God has decided to make us OR adopt us as his children. He has created us to accomplish his will, and he has sought us out to reconnect with him. If your dreams are aligned with God's desires for you, that is good news because he made you to accomplish those dreams!

If your dreams have not come true in the past, you might wonder, "Why should I believe this now?" Good question— and one we human beings don't totally understand. But we do know that the Bible says some things about that.

First, it is a pattern for God's people to be in slavery and misery at the hands of others or because of their own choices and then for God to deliver them. That was the entire story of the Israelites. They were in slavery and even gave up thinking life could be different. But God did fulfill their dreams for deliverance and a promised land. Similarly, when Jesus came, he said he came to seek the lost sheep and restore the things that were lost. Why did God allow the Israelites to be lost for so long? We don't know. But we do know that after that period of lostness, he entered into lives and restored them. So, you are not the first one who has wondered why God has seemingly been absent from your life for a while.

Second, sometimes we have to grow and mature into dreaming the dreams that fit us, as we shall see. My four-year-old wants to drive my car. It is her dream. But right now the father says, "No, that dream doesn't fit you. How about a bike?" or "Great dream! Just remain faithful, and I'll let you do that when you're ready." Similarly, sometimes our dreams haven't happened because, in his wisdom, God has said no; perhaps he wants us to mature a bit first.

Third, sometimes our dreams haven't happened because we have strayed and not done life according to God's ways. The Israelites did not find the Promised Land for a long time past when they should have if only they had listened and obeyed—and we are the same way. Sometimes we have not gotten with the program.

Fourth—and this is one of the hardest reasons of all to accept—sometimes people have destroyed our dreams. That is a theme in the Bible as well, and this reality does not negate that God is there to deliver us and help us realize our dreams. For some reason, though, he sometimes allows evil to win a battle in our lives, but he will always win the war.

So, I understand if you have doubts. That's OK. God understands your doubts; he wrote the book that has all the experiences we just mentioned. So, if you have doubts, you fit right in. But know that, in that same book with stories of lost dreams, shattered dreams, sin, rebellion, immaturity, and all the rest, *there is the big message that God is on your side and you can trust him no matter what has happened.* He is still God, and he is in control right now.

1. Do you see yourself as someone designed by God to "make it"? Why or why not? Describe a specific time when you have succeeded because of a God-given talent or ability.

2. Rewrite Ephesians 2:10 in the space below, substituting *I* or *me* each time the verse says *we* or *us.*

3. How do you feel about being God's workmanship, created to do good things? How is that perspective different from the way others have treated you?

4. Do you believe God delights in your well-being? Have you ever had someone else delight in your doing well? If you never told that person how much his or her encouragement has meant to you, do so!

5. Meditate on this verse: "[God] satisfies your desires with good things so that your youth is renewed like the eagle's" (Psalm 103:5). You are someone God wants to satisfy with good things, because he loves you.

6. Think about—and ask God to help you see—what stands in the way of your believing that you are a person God wants good things for. What has kept you from seeing that? Why is it important to see that you qualify for good things, not because you have behaved or performed well enough, but just because God has decided that you do?

Memory Verse

Yet the LORD *longs* to be gracious to you;
 he rises to show you compassion.
For the LORD is a God of justice.
 Blessed are all who wait for him!
  — ISAIAH 30:18 (emphasis added)

DAY 3

Uncover Your Dreams

Sometimes when I speak, I ask the audience to look around at the building we are in. Usually these meeting places are large spaces, like conference centers or auditoriums, that involve quite complex architecture. I ask the audience to look at the beams, at the construction of the roofline, and then to join me in being amazed at the reality that the building actually works, that the beams are able to support all of that weight and remain steadfast and sturdy. When the audience really focuses on the building and its grandeur, I ask them, "Where did this building come from?"

They answer, "From a builder," or "From an architect." While that is true, I ask them to think a little deeper, because that architect came from somewhere. The answer I'm after? The heart and soul of a little child. Many years ago, a little child somewhere noticed that when she played with blocks or made simple pencil drawings, something came alive in her. Doing those things excited her more than playing with soccer balls. When she drew or built little towers, her whole being came alive.

What caused that? A talent, a gift. That talent in her little heart and soul was put to use as she developed it, went to school, practiced, and matured. Then, one day many years later, from the talent of that little girl, a magnificent building was born.

In the same way that the architect began with a talent, an ability, and nurtured it, you too have gifts, talents, and desires resting in your soul. Some are for tasks, like drawing or building; others may be for relationships. But, sadly, it is possible to bury talents in the ground or at least lose touch with them. It is also possible not to use your talents out of fear or because you're too busy.

But even before you can embrace your talents and invest them in some pursuit, you have to know what they are. Have you ever really thought about what you love to do? What makes you feel alive? What kinds of abilities seem to just bubble up from your soul and catch your interest? I'm not just referring to activities you would want to do for work or as a career, but even hobbies or unrealized dreams. Those desires may be windows into your soul, revealing your treasure chest of talents and gifts. Today, I want you to look inside and see what you find.

Ask God to help you as you think about the following questions:

1. When you were a child, what did you do with your free time?

2. What were your favorite toys and experiences?

3. When did you get the best responses from those around you? What were you doing?

4. What activities made you so happy that you'd lose track of time?

5. If you had to choose one thing to do every day for the rest of your life—and if money were no object—what would you do?

6. If you knew you were going to die in one year, how would you want to spend your last year?

7. What activities come easily to you?

8. What do you find yourself daydreaming about doing? What does that answer say about what you love? What does it say about what you are good at?

9. Based on what you have learned from answering these eight questions, are you ready to write down your dream? Do so now. Note what talent, gift, or ability your dream involves.

DAY 4

Identify Your Relationship Dreams

Sometimes when we think about dreams and goals, we automatically think of a certain career, a specific hobby, or a precise goal. For instance, you might think, *I've always wanted to be an interior designer, I've always wanted to get my pilot's license, I want to lose fifty pounds, I want to overcome my depression,* or *I want to sail around the world.* When we begin to talk about our talents, activities naturally come to mind.

But relationship dreams are also very important. And just as it is possible to give up on seeing yourself as someone who could have a certain kind of job, it's also possible to give up on seeing yourself as someone who could have a certain kind of relationship. You may have even come to believe that you are unlovable.

So take a moment to think about what relationships you wish you had. Who would you like to know better? What other people would you like to have in your life? How would you like for them to treat you? Your answers to these questions reveal your relationship dreams.

Are there things that you want in your relational world that you have not been able to achieve? Here are some possibilities:

- You are single and want to have a richer dating life
- You are single and desire to find a meaningful relationship or marriage
- You are married and want your marriage to be better
- You want to experience friendships that are deeper and more meaningful
- You want to overcome relationship patterns that have been keeping you from being fulfilled either personally or professionally
- You want to develop a support team of people to walk through life with you
- You want to find a coach or mentor and establish a meaningful relationship that helps you grow

TAKE A LOOK

In the same way that you looked inside yourself to identify some of your other dreams and goals, look inside your heart and ask God to show you a relationship goal that you have as well.

1. If you could change anything about your relationship life, what would it be?

2. What has kept you from making that change? Is that a good reason? Why or why not?

3. What kind(s) of relationships are you lacking in your life right now?

4. When, if ever, have you had that kind of relationship? What was it like?

5. When, if ever, have you tried to establish that kind of relationship? If you have, what happened? If you haven't, why not? And if you have but you aren't trying now, why did you give up?

6. Have you ever thought about the fact that God can help you fulfill those relationship dreams? Why is that truth significant?

Read this verse and note your response:

God places the lonely in families.

— PSALM 68:6 (NLT)

7. What kind of family do you desire? A support community? A family of friendships? A spiritual community? Something else?

8. Describe your ideal relationship life.

DAY 5

Distinguish between Dreams and Fantasies

There is a difference between a dream and a fantasy. A real dream is meant to come to fruition, but fantasies are just mental escapes or idle musings. We don't pursue them. However, here is an important fact: many real dreams that could become reality go the way of fantasy because we attack them as soon as we think of them. Let's make sure that your dreams don't immediately get shut down by this very familiar process.

Here is what happens to many people who do not realize their dreams. They look into their souls, and they see what they desire. They think what life would be like if that dream were a reality. They relish it. But then a voice inside or a memory intrudes and says something like this:

- *Why am I even thinking of this? It will never happen.*
- *I've tried that before, and it didn't work. There's no chance for it to happen this time.*
- *I could never pull this off. I'll just embarrass myself.*
- *I don't have the money to do that.*
- *I'm not smart enough to do that.*
- *Stop thinking that could happen. You're wasting your time.*

When we have thoughts like these, the dream is abandoned to the realm of fantasy. It becomes an idle wish that we will never act on; it will never find its fulfillment in the real world. And what just occurred inside our head is usually like something that happened to us in real life: our dreams were put down by a real person, and now that criticism is reenacted inside our head even without people present. The result is the same: our dream is judged and abandoned. It dies.

We will deal with this dynamic in the coming days. But now, very early on, I want you to notice whether it is occurring in your mind. So write down what happens inside of you as you look for your buried dreams. I do *not* want you to give up on your dream or goal without even realizing that you may have shut it down. I do *not* want you to allow those voices or false beliefs to keep you stuck in the same rut, not fully utilizing the talents and abilities God has given you.

Look inside yourself and notice:

1. When you saw or started to uncover your dream, what did you feel?

2. Either right when you saw your dream, right after, or since then, what have you begun to feel and think about it? Did your emotions go from excitement to discouragement? Did your enthusiasm begin to wane?

3. If you found yourself discouraged and unenthusiastic, why did that happen? What were you thinking or telling yourself about your dream?

4. What did you begin to see as the obstacles to realizing your dream? When you saw the obstacles, what happened inside?

5. Get very specific about what these internal obstacles are and write them down.

At this point, we don't have to deal with each of the specific obstacles. But you must be aware that this behavior is happening, or it will steal your dream. The Bible says that the forces of darkness come to steal your life (John 10:10), and this is one of the ways that it happens. Negativity, fear, past hurt, and false beliefs can all keep you imprisoned. Notice if this is happening—and *keep going* anyway. Instead of obeying those voices this time, just notice them and do this:

> Realize that those voices are part of the process. If you were traveling in an airplane and hit turbulence in the air, you wouldn't turn off the engines and let the plane fall to the ground. So don't do that with your dream! The negative voices in your head are just turbulence in your flight toward your dream. Notice it, but do *not* land the plane before you even take off.

PART TWO

Figure Out Your Dream

DAY 6

Act in Line
with Your Abilities

One of my favorite stories Jesus told is the parable of the talents. You can read it in Matthew 25:14–30. It teaches us many lessons about reality.

First, the master entrusts talents to people and then goes away on a journey. In other words, he gives them the resources to accomplish something and then sets them free to do it. He lets them choose whether or not they are going to do anything with their lives, and God gives us that same choice. What incredible trust God has granted you with the gift of your life!

Second, the people react to the master's gift in different ways, and the same happens in real life. Some people have a plan and use their talents and resources to do good things; they multiply the impact of their gifts. Others bury their talents in the ground of inactivity and passivity just like one character in the story did. Not surprisingly, nothing happens in these people's lives.

However, there's a third point that I want to focus on today: each person was given a different amount of talents and had different abilities.

To one he gave five talents of money, to another two talents, and to another one talent, each according to his ability. Then he went on his journey.

(Matthew 25:15)

Similarly, God has given you a certain amount of ability and talents (resources). They will not be the same as what other people have, because they don't need to be. God has given you what you need to do what he created you to do. Your part is to recognize your talents and abilities and then use them.

Your dream, for example, might be to start your own business. What are your abilities? One person who has that dream begins a huge company with millions of dollars of venture capital because she has the ability to do that kind of big deal. Another person begins a tutoring business out of her home for children in the community. Both uses of their God-given talents are valid, and both people are blessed by God for using their gifts. One person uses her singing talent to become a professional opera singer, and another joins the church choir. Both uses of their God-given talents are valid, and both singers use the amount of ability that they have been given. The key is to match what you try to do with the talent and amount of ability you have.

The Bible is very clear about the fact that we all have different abilities and different gifts, and we should have a very good and accurate understanding of what those abilities and gifts are. Again, I may have a dream to play professional basketball, but at 5′10″ and at my age, I need to realize that God has chosen a different path for me.

Hear what the apostle Paul wrote:

> For by the grace given me I say to every one of
> you: Do not think of yourself more highly than
> you ought, but rather think of yourself with sober
> judgment, in accordance with the measure of faith
> God has given you. Just as each of us has one body
> with many members, and these members do not
> all have the same function, so in Christ we who
> are many form one body, and each member
> belongs to all the others. We have different gifts,
> according to the grace given us.
>
> (ROMANS 12:3–6)

So be realistic about your abilities and don't compare yourself
to others. No one else has your life, and your comparisons will
never be helpful (see Galatians 6:4–5). Instead, look at your
own abilities and talents, and see if your dreams and aspira-
tions fit who you are. Ask your friends, because they may
know you and your gifts and abilities better than you do. Get
feedback. If I wanted to join the NBA, I hope my friends
would say to me, "Get real!" But if I said to them, "I could
never become a psychologist and write books," I'd like to
think they would say, "What is your problem? Of course you
could! Get off your duff and get to work!"

Today, use the following questions to get real about what
you are thinking of accomplishing:

1. Is your dream in line with your abilities or is it a fantasy? You may need to remind yourself that just because you have never done something before doesn't necessarily mean it's impossible. You may have never been in good physical shape, but you could still get there. However, if your dream has nothing to do with your ability or experience, it may be a fantasy not worth pursuing. In the lines below, list the talents that are required for your dream to become a reality. Do you have these abilities? Which abilities do you need to develop or want to sharpen?

2. Make a list below of the people who want you to succeed and who will be honest with you. Ask them if pursuing your dream makes sense. Do not ask negative people who will discourage you (a point we will cover later). Ask those who really want to help and will have something honest and constructive to say.

3. Ask God to show you about your dreams and your talents. He created you and has a lot invested in your making the right choice. You might want to write your prayer to him in the space provided.

4. You may want to pursue a more formal way of finding out if your dream is right for you. Vocational counselors, career counselors, health experts, psychologists, business managers, and perhaps even elders in your church may be available to counsel you on what is required to achieve your dream and whether it seems to fit the talents and abilities God has given you.

DAY 7

Unearth the Talent Buried in the Ground

As we saw yesterday in the parable of the talents, the man with one talent buries his talent in the ground. When questioned by the master, he says that he was afraid, so he buried his talent. Afraid of failing and afraid of the master, this man went into protective mode. He wanted to preserve the little that he had and not risk getting hurt.

You can probably relate to that feeling of not wanting to fail or get hurt. You know that you have dreams and desires, but you have long since buried them. But have you ever really dealt with the fears that led you to bury your dreams in the first place? Have you ever asked yourself why you did that?

It may be helpful to figure out what prompted you to hide your talents in the ground. Then you can get past those fears, knowing that those experiences and people are in the past and don't have to have that kind of power over you anymore.

1. What person, if any, was behind your decision to not try anymore to achieve your dream? Who hurt you?

2. What series of events led you to give up on your dreams? What happened?

3. Have you ever sought healing for the pain those events caused? If you haven't, find someone to talk to and, if needed, get professional help. Sometimes the events and hurts that cause us to give up can be very painful and need some very specialized help.

4. If you were interacting with an unsafe person, it is important to let go of the voices that person left in your head, the beliefs that you accepted as true because of that relationship. Combat those voices and beliefs on a moment-by-moment basis. First, figure out what they are and write them down. Now replace them with positive statements.

We'll talk later about how to set up supportive relationships to undo what these past relationships have done to you. You need new voices in your head—supportive ones and healing ones. You need safe people you can call when you want truth and encouragement.

DAY 8

Play the Movie

People who reach their goals are usually not special in the ways we tend to think they are. We look at people who accomplish great things and think, *Wow, I wish I could have done that. She must be so gifted or talented or smart to have done that. I wish I had those abilities.*

Sometimes, in the cases of extreme and unusual accomplishment, the person does have remarkable gifts or talents. These people are the superstars. For example, there are few voices like Bono's and few complete golfing packages like Tiger Woods. These are the exceptions. A lot of accomplished musicians and golfers, for example, certainly have talent, but not the amount that a Bono or a Woods possesses. But even without superstar talent, these folks are dream-reachers because they accomplish great things in their own right. Now, here is the fascinating part: there are thousands of other people who have just as much ability as the dream-reachers but they never accomplish anything with that ability. These people are the sleepers; they've buried their talents in the dirt. They don't recognize that success is often more about practice, habits, patterns, and motivation than ability.

So how does one become a dream-reacher rather than a sleeper? One of the most important practices I've learned from dream-reachers has nothing to do with talent or ability. It is what I call "Play the Movie." Here's how it works.

Dream-reachers look at everything they do and play the movie forward to see what results that action will probably produce at a later time. Then they decide whether or not they would like those consequences. Finally, they let the realization of those later results *really sink in,* and it motivates them to either do that action or do something else. Quite simply, they ask themselves, "If I do this, what does the future look like? Do I like that picture?" They see their current action as a scene in a larger movie, and they play the movie forward to see if they like the ending. The resulting motivation is one of the big reasons why dream-reachers accomplish their goals. They look at taking a class, for example, and play that forward. They see that if they take that class and another one and another, then at the end of the movie is a college degree. Other dream-reachers consider working out when they feel terrible, and they play that forward. Then, they see the weight disappearing and the physical fitness increasing. That picture motivates them to go forward.

Now is the time for you to begin thinking like a dream-reacher. Here's how it works:

Look at what you have been or are doing to reach your goals. Here are some possible answers:

- You have fantasized about your dreams, but never taken them seriously.
- You have thought about your dreams, but never taken the first steps to get help accomplishing them. You may do so "someday."

- You took a step toward one of your dreams, but when you did, you got discouraged and gave up.
- You've thought about your dreams but allowed others to discourage you or sidetrack you with their agenda.

OK, now I want you to do what dream-reachers do: play the movie. Play the movie forward from where you are right now and what you have been doing and see where it takes you. In other words,

If you continue to do the same thing you are doing now, what will happen to your dream? What will your life look like if you continue doing what you have been doing?

Now, see that reality. If you continue to do what you are doing now, that means that you will not have what you want—like that new job, or career, or hobby, or experience, or body, or relationship, or improved relationship. If you continue to do what you have been doing, you are signing up for the same result that you have been getting.

Now, let that truth sink in. What does that feel like? For example, if you continue to withdraw, or think negatively, or pull back, then you already know where that will get you, and I bet you don't like it. There is your motivation to change. So, it's time to do something different.

As you go forward, keep that movie playing. When you want to quit, play the movie. When the going gets difficult, play the movie. When you don't know what to do and want to give up, play the movie. It will drive you. When you see the negative outcome, you will get moving and do something different. When you see the positive outcome, you will keep moving as you see your dream within reach. You will begin to taste that possibility, and that reality will keep you moving forward.

Ask yourself these questions:

1. Based on your talents and abilities, what dreams have you considered but never achieved?

2. What do you feel when you think about taking specific, concrete steps toward realizing your dreams?

3. What will your life look like if you don't make a change, if you keep going on your current path?

4. How do you feel about that possible outcome? Is that what you want your life to look like?

5. Now play the movie forward with each of your dreams. Which one creates an outcome that really excites you? Which one has realistic, positive consequences? Describe that dream here.

6. What will you feel like if you achieve this dream? What will your life look like?

Now, let those realities sink in—and then get moving to make things different than they have been.

If you think about the future and it's depressing, that is actually good. That depression is a red flag that shows you it's time to do something different. It does *not* mean that your life has to turn out that way. It just means you have to do something different. That is the key lesson of Play the Movie: it's time for you to do something different. Keep that play-the-movie motivation ever before you. Keep it in the forefront of your mind.

DAY 9

Get Specific about Your Dream

One reason a lot of people never achieve their dreams is that they are not specific about what those dreams are or about what life would look like if those dreams actually came true. For example, "I want a better life" is not a specific or measurable dream to pursue. "I want a deeper connection with my spouse" is not very specific either. "At some regular interval, I want to spend an evening with my spouse talking about our deepest feelings, fears, desires, goals, and dreams" is much more doable: it's a dream that's specific enough to pursue.

But there are many reasons why people are not usually specific: fear of being held accountable to their goal, being out of touch with what they want, and fear of failing are three. No matter what your reason, if you don't know where you are going, you probably won't get anywhere. Having a specific definition of what you want is important. It commits you and defines the path for getting there.

So, write down the dream you considered yesterday and what life will look like when it has happened. Describe your dream in a way that is measurable. "I want a better dating life" is not measurable; "I want to go on two dates a week" is measurable. "I want to lose fifty pounds" tells us a lot more than "I want to get in shape."

Next, set a deadline for reaching that goal. "I want to be going on two dates a week by June" is a timeline that will help you organize the things you need to do to make your goal happen by then. "I want to get a bachelor's degree by 2010" will tell you how many courses you need to take each semester. And "I want to have assets totaling $750,000 by 2015" will tell you the annual growth rate that you have to meet.

Make sure that your goal is actually achievable—but I don't mean that you are to dream small. I mean make sure you are being rational as you define your dream. Going to the moon might be an exciting dream, but going on a vacation around the world is more apt to happen in our lifetime (unless you are on your way to astronaut training). Dreaming of being richer than Bill Gates is not as likely to happen as getting out of debt and becoming financially independent by a certain year. People do that all the time, whereas few people do what Mr. Gates has done. So pick something that is in the realm of possibility even if it has never been done before. Remember the Wright Brothers when you dream, but don't expect to become Superman.

1. What is it you actually want to see happen in your life?

2. Now write it down: "I want to _____ by _____ (a date)."

3. How badly do you want to see your dream become reality? What are you willing to do in order to achieve this goal?

4. Place a statement of your dream somewhere you will see it often.

5. Pray something like this: "God, here is my dream. Please help me become the person who can attain this—and please provide me with the resources I'll need to accomplish it. I yield myself to you, and if there is something about this dream that I need to know, I trust you to show me. If my dream is too small, let me know. If it is too large, tell me that also. If it is the wrong dream for me right now, please close the door. If it is your dream for my life, I place it in your hands and trust you to help me bring it about."

DAY 10

Lay One Brick at a Time

All dream-reachers accomplish their goals the same way, and it's the only way: one little step at a time. A wall is built one brick at a time. A client list is built one phone call at a time. A hundred pounds is lost one forty-five-minute exercise session at a time. A hard body is built one sit-up at a time. A good relationship is built one sacrifice, one conflict resolution, or one act of forgiveness at a time.

Sleepers who do not accomplish things look at dream-reachers and think those people possess something, some superhuman ability, that they simply don't have. Sleepers don't realize that *everyone* works the old-fashioned way: one step at a time.

Your job is to figure out what the "bricks" are for your dream. You may not think you can build a wall, but anyone can pick up a brick and stack it on another one. So, you have to figure out what the little steps are that will get you there. If you want to lose fifty pounds, the little steps are probably something like these:

- Go for a brisk forty-five-minute walk today. Do it again tomorrow. And the next day. And every day after that.

- Go to a meeting like Weight Watchers at least once a week.

- Make a daily call to a supportive person who holds you accountable.

- Join a structured program that outlines for you the exercise/weight-loss plan you need to follow.

- Each day write down what you eat.

- Have a day-by-day plan for talking out your emotions with someone instead of eating over them.

- Call someone when you are tempted to eat.

None of these things is a superhuman task. You can do every single one of them—and you must do them to reach your dream. But most people don't ever know that success is that simple, or they would do it. Realizing dreams involves small steps, taken one at a time. You just have to figure out what the steps are.

1. What are the very small and doable steps you need to take to accomplish your goal?

2. What do you need to do to get ready to take the first step?

3. Who will help you take these steps? Different people may be helpful at different points.

4. Most people who don't get to their goal right away cannot be satisfied with very small steps, so they don't do them, yet those steps are the very things that could get them where they want to be. Do you agree with that statement? Why or why not? How do you feel about taking such small steps that may not seem to get you any closer to your goal?

Memory Verse

Go to the ant, you sluggard;
consider its ways and be wise!
It has no commander,
no overseer or ruler,
yet it stores its provisions in summer
and gathers its food at harvest.
— Proverbs 6:6–8

PART THREE

⟿ Plan Ahead ⟿

DAY 11

Create a Plan

Many people get excited and all juiced up about accomplishing a goal or fulfilling a dream, but too often after the initial excitement, nothing really happens. Why? Fear of failure, lack of motivation, insufficient support . . . or another very important one: the lack of a plan.

If you are going to get from point A to point B, how are you going to do it? It is not just going to happen. You need a plan to execute, a particular path to follow.

What is *your* plan?

How are you going to do it?

What steps will get you to your goal?

As the saying goes, the plan works if you work the plan. If you want to improve your dating life, how are you going to do that? Hire a coach, join a service, find an accountability partner, read books that deal with the fear of rejection, attend three social events a week—these could be parts of a plan to get you there. If you want to retire at age fifty and you are thirty years old, finding and buying three rental properties a year is an example of a plan that might help you reach your goal. There are as many right plans as there are good ideas, and a specific plan is necessary to turn any idea into reality.

Today, think about your plan:

1. As you think about your goal or dream, brainstorm some of the steps that could help get you there. List them here:

2. Review the steps you wrote above. Are these steps appropriate for you at this stage? Why or why not? What research and education might also help you determine future steps?

3. Are the steps you've outlined enough to help you reach your goal? Are they challenging enough? Do they stretch you? Overall, how do you feel about your plan?

4. Think through each step you've listed and what you might need to get from one to the next. Do they logically lead you to achieving your goal? Are they in the right sequence? If not, consider a different order.

5. List below the names of people or organizations to whom you can submit your plan for feedback. Who knows something about what you are trying to do? Who can look at your plan and tell you if it is sound?

6. A plan works if you work the plan. Are you committed to working this plan? But what difficulties do you usually encounter whenever you tackle a new task? What can you do to keep from getting derailed this time?

7. Write down your plan—with all the steps arranged in a logical order—now. You may need a special document or journal if your plan is extensive, or you could outline it here. The important thing is that your plan is written down.

DAY 12

Plan the Critical Path

Goals and dreams have a direction just like a journey. If you are driving from New York to California, you don't just get in the car and drive (unless you're eighteen and have never done that before!). Instead, you think in terms of segments: "If I leave on Monday morning, I want to make it to _____ by Monday evening. Then by lunch on Tuesday I want to be in _____." And so on. You know which cities you have to get to by what time in order to reach your goal by the desired target date.

Similarly, if I'm writing a book, if the manuscript is due by a certain date, and if it needs to be 100,000 words long, I can't just sit down and write as the mood hits me. (Oh, for that kind of life!) Instead, I have to figure out how many months I have and how much time I have each week to spend on the project, and then I do the math to determine how many words I have to finish each week in order to meet the deadline. Otherwise, I will never get there. Then, I have to monitor my progress along the way and adjust. If I am ahead, I can take a little time away. If I am behind, I have to keep driving and skip some sightseeing that day to make it to the next milestone. Otherwise, I will miss arriving at my destination when I need to.

I call this plan a "critical path." It is a linear look at time with markers along the way that say, "This has to be done by this date in order for the next step to happen by a certain date. All of that has to happen along the way in order for the goal to be reached."

If people are building a house, they chart the plan this way: "The foundation has to be laid by a certain date. The framing has to be finished by another date. The dry-walling has to be done by another date."

When you plan in chunks like that, you get the job done. Otherwise you're just looking at a too-big-to-deal-with goal that goes nowhere. You have no idea where you are, and the pieces cannot come together.

Another example of a critical path is the Weight Watchers program. If you are counting your points each and every day, you know what you have in reserve, or where you are over the line. That will tell you whether or not you can eat that cake the next day. Companies manage their cash flow the same way. Virtually every successful venture has this kind of plan behind it. Now it's time to get yours together.

1. What is the target date for your goal? When do you want your dream to be reality? (See Day 9: "Get Specific about Your Dream" to see the deadline you originally set for yourself.)

2. Review the steps your dream will require. (See Day 11: "Create a Plan.") Next to each step, write how much time it will take. Be sure to allow some time for unexpected delays.

3. Add up the time for each step. This will give you the total time involved in accomplishing your dream.

4. Subtract the total time your plan requires from your target date. When do you need to start? Is this timing realistic? Do you need to adjust your target date?

5. Who will hold you accountable to your timeline?

6. Get a planner, a calendar, a notebook, or some other tool and write down what has to be done by when. Review it and, when you're satisfied, give a copy to your accountability partner.

Memory Verse

There is a time for everything,
and a season for every activity under heaven.
– Ecclesiastes 3:1

DAY 13

Determine What Has to Go

Fact: you can't do it all. There just is not enough time, energy, or resources for you to do everything that you want to do in life. So, for you to accomplish your goal, some activities and involvements are going to have to go away. For example, if you look at the plan I had for writing this book (see Day 21: "Monitor External Forces"), I had to give up weekend social activities for six months. There is only so much time, and something had to go. Oh, how I missed playing golf for that long! But I wanted to achieve my dream of writing this book even more than I wanted to golf.

If you are going to get out of debt and pay off those credit cards, for example, that morning latte that costs you $100.00 a month may have to go away for a while, along with some other things. But play the movie forward and think what happens to your goal if you continue that morning ritual. It dies. Yet what happens if you forgo that cup of coffee? You'll be one step closer to getting out of debt.

Jesus said that if we are to reach a particular goal we have to first count the costs (Luke 14:28–33), or we will get halfway to the goal and not make it. Reaching your goal is going to cost you. Period. But if your goal is a good one, achieving it will be worth the costs. If your goal has real value—value that brings life—then sacrificing to attain it is definitely worthwhile. Just know that there is going to be sacrifice involved.

And the reason is simple. You cannot have two things in the same space. You can't spend the same dollar on coffee and paying off your credit cards. You can't have the same energy for two projects that are all-consuming. You are going to have to decide what to let go of in order to reach your goal.

Whenever I consider doing something new, I have a friend who says to me, "So, what are you going to let go of in order to be able to do that?" Great question, especially because I don't normally think that way. I tend to just add things to my life, but if I don't subtract things in order to pay for the ones I add, the new ones will not happen.

1. What is competing for your time as you consider what accomplishing your dream will require? Which of those sources of competition can you give up?

Sometimes we can't give up things that are competing with our dream. For example, your goal may be going back to school and finishing a degree, but if you have young children and school would take you away from them too much, then the timing for your dream may not be right. Your children are more important. But if you can cut something, it may be worth doing so in order to reach your goal.

2. What nonessential activities in your current schedule may have to go?

3. What nonessential relationships may have to be put on hold?

4. What nonessential spending may have to stop?

5. What nonessential expenditures of energy may have to cease?

6. What nonessential time-eating activities may have to go away? Give up the nightly sitcom, for example, to ride the exercise bike instead.

7. Do an audit of the past month and how you spent your time, energy, money, passion, and other resources. You may be surprised at how much extra time, energy, money, passion, and other resources you can find once you begin eliminating those things that are robbing you of what you need in order to realize your dream.

DAY 14

Get Resources

Part of creating your plan is making sure you have adequate resources that will propel you to your goal. You have to pack your bags of supplies and make sure you have the resources you need to get there. Jesus put it this way:

> Suppose one of you wants to build a tower. Will he not first sit down and estimate the cost to see if he has enough money to complete it? For if he lays the foundation and is not able to finish it, everyone who sees it will ridicule him, saying, "This fellow began to build and was not able to finish."
>
> Or suppose a king is about to go to war against another king. Will he not first sit down and consider whether he is able with ten thousand men to oppose the one coming against him with twenty thousand? If he is not able, he will send a delegation while the other is still a long way off and will ask for terms of peace.
>
> (LUKE 14:28–32)

What are you going to need to reach your goal? Remember, God is not short on resources. He owns the cattle on a thousand hills. He has wisdom and people and angels that he can send you. Don't think that a goal is not achievable because of a lack of resources. Between you and God, those necessary resources can be found—but you may have to get busy and find them!

Today, you have to figure out what resources you're going to need to fulfill your dream:

1. Is your dream or goal going to require money? If so, how much? How much will that cost you in the long run? Where are you going to get this money?

2. Is your dream going to require new knowledge? If so, where are you going to get it? From people? organizations? libraries? churches?

3. If you don't know the answer to either one of the above questions, where are you going to begin looking for answers?

4. If you are going to need support, an alliance, or a partnership, whom do you trust enough to work with? Who shares your vision? Who has the knowledge and reliability to walk with you until your dream is reality?

5. Ask God to both lead you to the necessary resources and give you wisdom in making your decisions.

DAY 15

Seek Wisdom and Knowledge

Have you ever heard the expression "Don't reinvent the wheel"?

A lot of people have probably already traveled the path that you are now traveling. In fact, if you aren't looking for the unified theory of physics, then your goal is something that other people have accomplished. You don't have to discover how to do it for the first time in history. You don't have to reinvent the wheel.

But you may not know what those people know, and this step involves seeking the wisdom and knowledge that you do not possess. If you're trying to lose weight, for instance, learn how from the ones who have done that. If you're trying to get out of debt, go to a good financial counselor who knows how to help you do that. If you are overcoming a depression or a relationship problem, seek the knowledge that others with experience or expertise possess. Other people know how to do what you are trying to do. Your job is to go find out from them what they know, to learn from them the how-to's for what you are trying to do. The Bible says it this way:

Get wisdom, get understanding;
  do not forget my words or swerve from them.
Do not forsake wisdom, and she will protect you;
  love her, and she will watch over you.
Wisdom is supreme; therefore get wisdom.
  Though it cost all you have, get understanding.
Esteem her, and she will exalt you;
  embrace her, and she will honor you.
She will set a garland of grace on your head
  and present you with a crown of splendor.
                              (Proverbs 4:5–9)

With these verses in mind, answer the following questions:

1. Take an inventory of what you know about what you are trying to do. What have you been constantly wondering about that you don't have an answer to?

2. Who might know the answer to these questions?

3. Show your plan to people you trust and to experts in the field. Get their input on how you should adjust your plan to be realistic, thorough, and successful. Write their suggestions below:

4. Consider these sources of wisdom as well: classes, workshops, retreats, professionals, self-help groups, books, tapes, seminars, pastors, counselors, churches and other organizations that have programs for many different needs, online sources (classes and Web sites), the library, and experienced friends. Now go "get wisdom"!

PART FOUR

Protect Your Dream

DAY 16

Anticipate Obstacles

Be aware that, if you are going to accomplish anything significant, you are going to run into obstacles. (After all, if accomplishing your goal were easy, you would have already done so.)
But my guess is that you've probably even run into these
obstacles before. So now is the time to plan for them.

What do you see as standing between you and your dream?
What external factors have the capacity to derail you? We will
get to internal obstacles later, but for now, what obstacles in
the road before you are you going to have to deal with?

If you are going to build a house in the swamps of
Louisiana, for example, you are going to deal with poisonous
snakes and alligators, so you'd better be ready for them. If you
are going to start a Bible club in an elementary school, you are
going to run into people who hate any kind of faith. How will
you deal with them? If you are going to run into scheduling
conflicts with your job or your family responsibilities, how
will you resolve those?

People who don't reach their dreams have usually taken off
down a road, hit an obstacle, gotten discouraged, and quit.
But when planners hit an obstacle, either they've anticipated
it and are ready, or they are mentally prepared to creatively
overcome such obstacles. I want you to do both. Foresee what
you can, and adopt the mind-set that unexpected obstacles

will come and that's OK. Obstacles are just part of the path, and you will find a way to deal with them when you encounter them. Get ready for them; expect them.

1. Look through the steps of your plan again. As you think about each step, list in the left column below those obstacles that have the power to slow you down or stop you along the way.

Obstacles	Antidotes

2. In the right-hand column next to the obstacles, note how you can deal with each problem as it occurs. Feel free to include people and resources you can enlist to help you when—or even before—a problem arises.

3. Finally, don't be surprised when you have emotional reactions to the obstacles you encounter. Planning ahead may help reduce your shock, but obstacles are still

disappointing. How have you reacted to roadblocks in the past? What has helped you manage your emotions in the midst of adversity? What do you think you are going to feel when obstacles come? How will you deal with that feeling, whatever it is?

DAY 17

Assemble Your Team

In all of the research that has ever been done on people making positive changes in their lives, one factor has stood out. Following this one bit of advice is more likely to impact your success than almost anything else. This is the key:

Assemble a good team around you.

There is no such thing as a "self-made person." We all get wherever we are in life because of the help of other people. The converse is true as well: we often do *not* get to a desired place in life because of other people. People either help us make it happen, or they hinder us in some way. The implications of this truth are twofold.

First, if you are going to reach your goal, you need to get good people on your team. You need support, encouragement, feedback, wisdom, correction, information, guidance, experience, referrals, accountability, confrontation, and sometimes elbow grease. That list may sound long, but in reality, these are basic ingredients that any dream-reacher receives from a good support system. You may have heard about such systems without realizing it: they exist in groups ranging from Alcoholics Anonymous and Weight Watchers to divorce recovery to counseling to coaching to mentoring to the nuclear family. When people get together, they provide for each other what the individuals involved do not possess on their own, and they begin to accomplish things that otherwise would be impossible. There is a reason why people who have been addicts for years make progress after joining a support group. We were designed to get what we lack from others:

> Two are better than one,
>   because they have a good return for their work:
> If one falls down,
>   his friend can help him up.
> But pity the man who falls
>   and has no one to help him up!
> Also, if two lie down together, they will
>   keep warm.
>   But how can one keep warm alone?
> Though one may be overpowered,
>   two can defend themselves.
> A cord of three strands is not quickly broken.
>   (Ecclesiastes 4:9–12)

Second, you have to avoid allowing the people who stand in the way of your goal to continue to do that. If they have the ability to discourage you or stop you in some way, then they are not going to help; they are only going to hurt. We will deal with that issue on Day 19, but I just wanted to mention it now as you begin to consider the role of people in your journey.

So, who is going to be on your team?

1. Review the list below and think about the people you know or know of. Who could help you in the following areas?

   Support _____

   Encouragement _____

   Honest Feedback _____

   Wisdom and Experience _____

   Information and Guidance _____

   Referrals _____

   Accountability _____

   Time and Elbow Grease _____

2. Think through your own history. Do you tend to ask others for help? Why or why not? Do you accept help when people offer? Again, why or why not?

3. How do you expect people to respond to your request? Why? What fears do you need to face before you'll be able to ask for help?

4. Structure: What kind of help would be most beneficial? Do you need to join a group or find a counselor? Do you have a friend or a group of friends who will join you in pursuing your dream? Or perhaps you'll develop a "dream group," a circle of people who meet together to support one another? Do you have a prayer partner who will meet with you regularly? Can you get a few people who will be available to call for support or encouragement when you need it? List below the kind of help you plan to seek and use.

In the next section, we will look at how you can utilize the help of others particularly when you need it most. But right now I want you to think hard about the reality that you will need help. You will not be able to keep moving forward alone. You will not reach your goal alone. No one has ever succeeded alone, so don't fight the way God designed the universe. We all need each other.

DAY 18

Force Accountability

People reach their goals and dreams for one reason: they do what it takes to reach them. Now, that sounds like a little bit of a truism, but it is exactly right—yet living out that strategy can be difficult. Doing what it takes to reach our goals requires change, and we often don't like change. For example, when people want to lose weight, they must start exercising and change their eating habits. For any new skill to become easy, you must practice while it's hard. That presents a problem for most of us: we don't have the self-discipline to follow through on our own. We have a problem sticking to the plan.

On our own, we may get excited about change and even take a few steps to begin. Our initial excitement fuels the takeoff. Then the road gets difficult. We get uncomfortable. We hit an obstacle. We grow tired. That's when our lack of discipline does us in. Our plan to change goes the way of one more New Year's resolution. Fortunately, there's an answer— best illustrated by a familiar situation.

Who exemplifies lack of discipline? A young child. That's one reason why you don't send a three-year-old into the day expecting her to get herself dressed, fed, and ready for school. Instead, you provide the structure for that to happen. You set the schedule, give the specific tasks, and then hold her accountable. When she goes to preschool, the teacher does the same thing. You don't depend on the child to get through the day on her own.

To the degree that you do what feels good and what provides instant gratification, you resemble that child. Thus, you need similar structure to keep things on track. This is why companies have weekly management meetings to keep projects moving forward. This is why the IRS has an April 15 deadline with fines and penalties for late returns. We do not do what we don't like to do without structure.

So, if you are the kind of person who naturally has the discipline to utilize a support system, call those people every day, organize a weekly meeting, review your goals together, pray for one another, teach one another, correct one another, and do all the things we talked about yesterday, then great. You can structure your support team on your own. Go for it!

But if you are not the kind of person who tends to turn to others for support, then you are going to need more structure. You have to get your supportive friends to come together around an agreed-upon structure, or you need to join an already existing support group. Here are some options of both kinds:

1. Call a friend and covenant together to meet at a regular time to go over what you are doing and monitor your progress. Tell this friend that you want to be held accountable and supported as you walk this path.

2. Do the above with a small group of friends. Find between five and seven people who want to covenant together to meet at a regular time and support one another.

3. Get three friends together who will agree to a *daily* con-
    ference call to support one another in whatever each of
    you has to do that day to reach your goals. Get on the
    web or use a free conference-call service to communi-
    cate. Get up fifteen minutes earlier if it will give you the
    time you need to talk with each other every day.

4. Covenant together with a friend to touch base *daily*.
    When you are experiencing temptation of some sort
    and are about to bottom out, chicken out, or do some-
    thing that is going to hurt your chances of success, put
    in the 911 call to your friend right then.

5. Join an already existing structured group—Alcoholics
    Anonymous, Overeaters Anonymous, Weight Watch-
    ers, a recovery group at your church, a class at a local
    community college, an online dating service, etc. The
    key is that the group already exists, and its stated pur-
    pose is to help people like you.

6. Hire a coach or counselor or ask someone (a profes-
    sional or a volunteer) to mentor you. Set up a regular
    time to meet with that person.

7. Enroll in a structured degree program or a professional
    or vocational track at a school. If, for example, you want
    a real estate license, forget studying on your own.
    Instead, take a course. If you want to learn Spanish,
    enroll in a class. You are not listening to those tapes you
    bought for independent study, are you? So go sign up.

After twenty-five years of working with people in life
change, I am convinced that one of the biggest reasons for
failure is that people who need more structure do not get it.

Instead, they lie to themselves and say that they can reach their goals on their own. But they never do. The people who join an existing support group are the people who change. You can do it too. Just sign up. Today.

DAY 19

Steer Clear
of Unsafe People

In the Bible (Numbers 13 and 14), we find the story of the Israelites on the verge of setting out to claim the Promised Land. Moses sent a bunch of people ahead to get the lay of the land and ascertain the obstacles that lay before them. When this advance party came back, their report was not good. Many said there was no way Israel could conquer the land because the enemies were too strong and so many bad things could happen if they continued. The entire assembly was discouraged and wept. They also got mad at Moses for even having this idea in the first place.

But then two men stood up. Joshua and Caleb said no to the negative voices among them. They said the Promised Land could be conquered, and they saved the dream. If not for these two men, the negative voices would have killed the vision.

In your life, this same thing will happen. You will encounter enemies of your dream. They will tell you that it isn't possible, that you can't do it, that you're not smart enough, that it's too risky, or a million other excuses that can stop you in your tracks. Their motivations are many, but one key motivation that sets them apart from the Safe People in your life is that they are not concerned with what's best for you. For instance, they care more about how your actions will make them look or feel—weak, afraid, and unsuccessful. If you are achieving your goal, they will be more aware of their own weakness, fear, or lack of success, so they want to hold you back instead of feeling those things about themselves.

Clearly, these Unsafe People are afraid of taking their own steps, so they try to control yours. Your positive movement toward your dream may even feel threatening to them because it makes them think of their own dreams and failures. If they can squelch your enthusiasm, then they can feel comfortable in their own squelched existence. But if you move forward, you inadvertently make their stagnation more obvious. Or Unsafe People may care about your welfare but not have faith in your ability to change. Or they may just be negative, critical people.

Whatever the reason behind it, the negativity of Unsafe People often has nothing to do with you *and* nothing to do with reality. And these people are different from the people we mentioned earlier who are good, safe, supportive people whose feedback you need. Sometimes a negative word from Safe People is a gift, but negativity from Unsafe People is different. Unsafe People are not interested in you making it; they're often more interested in your *not* making it. So it is imperative that you avoid talking to Unsafe People about what you are doing.

We cannot eliminate all unsafe people from our lives. But we can avoid making ourselves vulnerable to their negativity and hurtfulness. As Proverbs says, "A prudent person foresees danger and takes precautions. The simpleton goes blindly on and suffers the consequences" (22:3, NLT). It is smart to hide your dream from the people who would endanger it. If you keep talking to them about it, you and your dream will suffer the consequences.

1. When have unsafe people discouraged you in the past? What was the effect on your dream or goals at the time?

2. Are those same people around you now? If not, are there others who have a similar effect on you? Who has the ability to bring you down and discourage you now?

3. Why do these Unsafe People in your life have that kind of power over you? What do you believe about them or about yourself that gives them that amount of power? What is it that you need from them that would be good to give up?

4. What are you going to do to protect your dream—and your path toward it—from the influence of Unsafe People? What specific boundaries do you need to set with them? How will you do that? Who can help you do that? Who can you call for support when you set and try to maintain those boundaries?

5. Do you need to talk about those boundaries with someone? If so, who?

DAY 20

Quarantine Your Weaknesses

We do not need new ways to fail. The old ones are working just fine.

Have you ever thought about that truth? We don't tend to fail in *new* ways. The weaknesses that derail us usually persist in our lives. Our patterns of failure tend to be pretty consistent over time. If we allow them to, these patterns will get us every time. That is why we don't need new ways of failing.

For example, if you've had a control problem that has destroyed a relationship in the past and you haven't dealt with that, then the same problem will destroy the next relationship. Or if you tend to be attracted to Unsafe People and get hurt, and you do not change that pattern, then you will probably pick another Unsafe Person and get hurt again. Or if you have worked toward goals in the past but, when you hit the first obstacle, have gotten discouraged and quit, that will happen again unless you change or prepare to deal with obstacles.

That's why one of the best things to do is *quarantine your weaknesses* in the same way that you would quarantine a disease. Your weaknesses will infect your dream and cause it to get sick and die if they are allowed to take over. So lock them up and prohibit their ability to spread.

Now, I don't know all of your failure patterns; only you do. But here are a few examples to show you what I'm talking about:

- If you hit an obstacle and then quit, get an accountability partner to report in to weekly or even more often. Tell that person about your tendency to withdraw when you hit an obstacle—and then, when you do hit an obstacle, talk with your partner and come up with other strategies instead of withdrawing and quitting.

- If you feel "all bad" even when you stumble just a little bit, tell someone about that tendency and then covenant with that person or group to call when you begin to feel that way. Then talk through your failure and sense of "all bad" so it doesn't derail you.

- If you tend to allow others to criticize you or talk you out of pursuing your dreams, then avoid sharing your dreams with those people, or simply stay away from them if they are too hurtful. If you have to see them, call your supportive people beforehand. Then deal with the difficult people and then call your support team afterward to debrief.

- If you have a pattern of not sticking to things that you start because of your lack of discipline, then do the kinds of things that we looked at in Day 18. Find the discipline and structure outside yourself and then let it keep you going.

- If you have derailed your weight loss by late-night carb binges, then don't have that food in your house. If you cannot *not* buy it when you shop, then only shop with a friend who will not allow you to buy it. Guard yourself.

You get the idea. Respect your failure patterns. They have gotten you before, and they will get you again if you don't pre-pare for them. But if you do, then you will win.

1. What are the ways that you have failed in the past? If you aren't sure, talk to the people who know you best and ask them. They can probably tell you.

2. Ask God to reveal the patterns that you need to change.

3. Before you begin down the same path again, plan your quarantine. Write below the strategies you could use to deal with this tendency to fail in the same way you've failed before.

Memory Verse

Guard your heart with all diligence,
  for from it flow the issues of life.
                — PROVERBS 4:23 (KJV)

PART FIVE

Implement Your Dream

DAY 21

Monitor External Forces

We talked earlier about the dysfunctional people, the Unsafe People, who can derail, if not destroy, your dreams and goals. That threat is easy to recognize. When these people hurt us, we feel it immediately in our hearts. But there is another threat that is just as deadly to a dream, but we don't see it as easily. It is more of a silent killer, and sometimes it can even be a "good" thing, though its effect on our dreams is not so good. What is this silent killer? Outside interference.

Outside interference happens when we are not careful to guard our time, energy, and focus. Too many other activities, time commitments, people, projects, etc. will crowd out time or energy that we could focus on our goals. You *cannot do everything*. You are going to have to learn to say no to some things and to exercise that "no muscle" when you encounter those outside forces and distractions.

This certainly does not mean that you drop out of life or break off all of your relationships. But it does mean that there are times when you get invited to something, or have an opportunity to do something, even fun or good, that will get you off task and derailed. For example, when I wrote my very first book—a dream that I had had for a while—I had to erect a very strong boundary against outside interference. Since I had a busy work schedule and could not take time off to write in the workweek, the only way to accomplish my goal was to guard the rest of my time. So, I made a rule: from 6:00 p.m. on Friday evening when I got off of work until Monday morning, I locked myself up in my house and could not do any outside activities except go out on Saturday night or to church. I did that for six months, and at the end of six months I had written *Changes That Heal*. That book began my journey down a publishing path, and I have now written over twenty books. But, had I not set that one boundary—that one simple monitor against external activities and other opportunities that always come our way—my dream of someday writing a book would never have happened.

Outside opportunities and other agendas, even good ones, will always be there, and you have to monitor how many of them you are going to accept so that your time and your focus on your goal remain solid.

1. What kinds of activities and distractions tend to just pop up and take your time and focus off of your goal?

2. Why do you have trouble saying no?

3. What people have the ability to distract you? Why do they have that power—and what can you do to take that power away from them? Do they know they are preventing you from achieving your dream?

4. What are you going to do to protect the time you need to fulfill your dream?

5. Do you need to explain this window of time to certain people? To whom do you need to say, "I am going to spend a certain amount of time working on this project and won't be available at that time to do what we normally do"—and when will you do that?

DAY 22

Get Comfortable
with Process

Consider this. If you were a farmer and your dream was to grow a big crop of corn, what would you do? You would do all the preparation we've been talking about, and then you would actually put the seed in the ground. Next, you would work the process while the corn is growing: weeding, irrigating, and protecting the fields would be your focus for months and months. You would *not* just get up every day and look into the field for corn. In the spring and early summer, you would not run into the field demanding that there be full ears of corn, getting mad or discouraged if there were not.

Can you imagine a farmer being angry at the plants on May 15 because they had produced no corn? What a crazy farmer he would be! But each day I see people approach very achievable goals the same way, and their unreasonable expectations derail them. They get on the scales one week after beginning their new program, and their weight is unchanged. They get discouraged, even angry at themselves or at the ones who sold them the program. They think, *This is never going to work. I will always be overweight.* So they go eat a large pizza. No corn in May, and it's all over.

The same thing happens when people try to develop a

portfolio of clients—or other assets, or income, or savings. People begin a program that would actually work and then look at the total too soon after they begin. They don't see themselves reaching the end goal fast enough, and they give up. Why?

They give up because *they do not understand process.* Things of value take time. Building a good relationship takes time. Getting in shape takes time. Making money takes time. By definition, time is a factor in everything that grows. Even a microwave takes some time to cook your dinner! God has built time into the equation of everything that we desire. If you are comfortable with that reality, you can succeed. If you are not comfortable with it, you cannot. You will demand immediate gratification and give up. So get used to the idea that realizing your goal is going to take some time.

1. How do you look at the ingredient of time? Do you see and accept it as necessary, or do you resent that it limits you? Do you believe God has given you enough time to do what he wants you to do?

2. How do you feel about the timeline it will take for you to achieve your goal? Is it discouraging? Does it make you want to give up? What truths can you speak against those feelings?

3. Do you value the process as much as the end result? What aspects of working toward your dream are fun? Are you engaged in the process? What could make the process even more enjoyable?

4. Look back and see what your impatience has cost you in the past. What did you feel when you didn't get quick results? What did you do? What would have happened had you kept going and not quit? Would you be across the finish line now? Don't you wish you had accepted the reality of time and kept going instead of being impatient?

5. Consider your patience level now. What might help increase your patience? Ask God to help you with your impatience. Pray for it. He calls patience "the fruit of the Spirit" (Galatians 5:22).

6. Talk over your tendency to "want it all now or give up" with a friend and figure out a way to get past that as time goes on.

7. Establish a timeline for your dream. How long should it take you to reach your goal? Look at what others have done to see if your timeline is realistic—and be sure to consult financial planners and weight-loss experts, not infomercials, when you're doing this research. Then accept the amount of time it will take to reach your goal.

Accept the reality that "it takes time." Get to be friends with time. It will bring you the fulfillment of a lot of dreams if you cooperate with it. Time is as real as gravity. Become friends with gravity and you can fly airplanes. Ignore it and you will crash. It is a good thing to learn how to use gravity *and* time.

DAY 23

Evaluate Your Progress and Your Heart

So, how is it going now that you are working toward your dream? Are you feeling empowered? Do you feel good about your plan and your progress? Can you see that this time is different?

Or are you losing interest again? Are you falling away early in your program? Do you see a familiar pattern?

If you're struggling, that is OK. In fact, it is normal, especially for people for whom the pursuit of dreams has been difficult. What I said about patterns of failure is very important, and their recurrence is very typical. So don't be surprised if yours is kicking in again. The key is to check in with yourself and stop old patterns in their tracks:

1. So, get real. Exactly where are you in the process? How is it going? How are you feeling?

2. If you are feeling good and seeing some progress, if you're feeling strong motivation to keep going, that's great. What has been fueling your enthusiasm? Figure out why it is working and what to do to keep that enthusiasm fueled.

3. If you are not feeling good about where things are, when did your momentum break down? Why? What did you do when you first began to feel discouraged—or what could you have done?

4. What negative patterns do you see yourself repeating?

This pattern has done you in before. Do *not* let it win again. Use the steps that we talked about in Days 17 and 18 to get it under control. Get help *now*. Reach out to the supportive people in your life; do not give up.

5. Turn back to Day 1, "Acknowledge the Source," and review the scriptures about God's view of you. Remember that God is for you, not against you. He wants you to do well, not see you fail.

DAY 24

Conduct a Spiritual Checkup

Remember the starting point of your journey? It was realizing that God is for you and will be involved in your dreams. From the very beginning, his design for humankind was always to do life *with* us. His plan from the start was to be in a relationship with us.

So how is your relationship with God going as you work toward your dreams? Are you remaining connected to him? Are you believing him for guidance and strength along the path?

God's part is to be faithful to us, and our part is to be faithful to him. Just like any relationship, that faithfulness includes a lot of elements. So today let's take a look at some components of our spiritual well-being as we pursue our goals and remain faithful to God along the way.

1. Abiding and Connecting: Jesus told us to abide in him, and that means to maintain a constant connection with him. How are you doing with that? Are you talking to him every day about your dream? What are you doing— or could you be doing—to stay connected with him about life as you go through every day?

2. Learning and Meditating on God's Word: Part of communicating with God and staying spiritually healthy and strong is spending some time every day in his Word. He speaks to us as we read the Bible, and it guides us and tells us how to get where we are going. How is your time in God's Word going? What time every day do you find—or could you make some time, even if it is just a little—to read, meditate, and be guided by his Word?

3. Praying for Others: Our spirituality was never meant to be self-centered. Part of our relationship with God involves our relationship with others and our concern for their concerns. Being involved in caring about others and taking them to God in prayer are activities of a healthy person. Which people that you care about do you pray for regularly? What things that God is doing around you and in the world are frequent topics of prayer?

4. Confession: God says that if we are doing things that we should not be doing, it will affect our connection to him, and he might not respond to our prayers until we wake up and change our ways. If we are doing things we should not be doing, God—like any parent—is not going to reward that behavior. He is going to want us to stop that and get on the right path. The Bible calls this wrong action "sin," and that word means to "miss the mark." In other words, if we are missing God's standard in some area of life, we need to turn around and behave differently. That is called "repentance."

    So, what do you need to confess to God and repent of today in order to be pure before him? What areas of your life have you been ignoring and need to come clean

about before him? He says that if you do, he will certainly forgive you and make you clean (see 1 John 1:9).
Also, it is important to confess those areas to someone
else so that you can be totally healed (see James 5:16)
and reassured that you are forgiven and accepted. Find
a safe person and have a good time of confession: come
clean before God. Whom will you confess to? When
will you call to schedule that time—and what are some
possible times you could meet?

5. Enjoying God: I like to think of worship as enjoying
   God and appreciating all of who he is. Worship is ado-
   ration, just getting into the wonder of God—his
   majesty, his incredibleness, his size, his character, and all
   of the other amazing aspects of who he is. Worship is
   being overwhelmed with him, like when someone falls
   in love and is overcome with the wonder of the other
   person. Enjoy your God every day. What do you do to
   worship and enjoy God each day?

6. Thanksgiving: Thankfulness does many things for us spiritually. It causes us to recognize God's role in making it all work, and it changes our whole outlook. It is a cure for negativity and actually makes us more successful and healthier. What are you thankful for? Are you telling God that every day?

7. Serving: A big part of being healthy and successful in life is to use our God-given blessings, gifts, and strengths to serve others. Service is to begin in our closest relationships and moves outward from there. Who are you serving? What are you doing—or could you be doing—that is not for you, but strictly for others?

8. Getting Healthy: *Holiness* is a tough word to relate to, but we followers of Christ are called to be holy people (see 1 Peter 1:16). Don't go buy any robes, but instead think about being holy this way: be whole. Being holy is basically about being healthy and about working out the kinks in our hearts, minds, and souls. In what ways—where and with whom—are you working on your issues and sin? These things *will* get in the way of being fruitful in life. So make sure you are on a growth path, working on the issues in your heart and in your relationships, and becoming whole. If you do that, life in general will improve.

DAY 25

Reward Yourself

No one can keep going without a break. The Bible talks about a Sabbath rest, for example, and contains many examples of parties and times to enjoy life. Today, it is time for you to do just that. Take today off from worrying about your goals and reward yourself for what you have been doing. Do something that you love—and don't worry about anything. Rest in God's care today, knowing that he is the guardian of your dreams.

One of the most important things we can ever learn is to rest in God and surrender the outcome of our efforts to Him. The Bible talks about that all the time, and it says that God even takes care of us while we sleep and counsels us, speaking to our mind, while we rest (Psalm 16:7). God says that if we are seeking him, the rest of life is going to take care of itself (see Matthew 6). So, today, give it a rest—but give it the kind of rest that a little child does: in the lap of her Father. Let him handle your worries today.

1. Are you good at letting go and not worrying? Why or why not? Are you good at rest and recreation? Why or why not? Would your friends and family agree with your assessment?

2. What do you do that replenishes you—and how often do you make time for that?

3. What can you do today that will refresh and renew you?

Make handing over your worries and plans to God an act of the will; let them go.

PART SIX

~∞ Move Forward ∞~

DAY 26

Take Time
for a Reality Check

As we've talked about, many components are involved in reaching a dream. One of them is the suitability of the dream, its size, and how well it matches who you are. Timing, obstacles, and available resources are other factors. Now that you are well along the path toward fulfilling your dream, let's take a reality check. There is nothing wrong with regrouping as you walk your dream path. In fact, readjusting your course can actually save your dream in the end.

1. How is your pursuit of your dream going so far? Are you on the right track? What makes you think so? Be specific.

2. Do you feel like your dream is a good fit for you? Why or why not?

3. Do you need to rethink the size or scope of your dream? Why or why not? Did you, for instance, bite off more than you can chew? Were you thinking too big, or do you just need to get some help?

4. Is your dream big enough? Or in what ways did you underestimate your abilities, resources, or talents? What might be an appropriate expansion of your dream?

5. Are there more obstacles than you expected? What unexpected obstacles have arisen? How are you dealing with them?

6. In what ways, if any, do you need to adjust your time-line? Be specific.

7. Are your self-defeating patterns too strong right now? What step do you need to take to deal with those patterns and get healthy before pursuing your goal? Be specific—and get help if you need it.

8. Who is going to help you assess your progress and either encourage you to keep going or help you make a course correction?

DAY 27

Enjoy an Inspiration Day

It gets tough reaching dreams. We run out of steam. We get tired and discouraged. We can easily begin to believe that we can't succeed. Sometimes, life is just hard.

We all need inspiration. Many sources of inspiration are available, but few are as powerful as the stories of those who have made it, who have done exactly what you want to do. There is a reason why infomercials have those people popping up on the screen, saying, "I was homeless and broke until I found this program. Now I am a millionaire." Not to give credibility to those schemes, but there is a reason why people pick up the phone and dial the 800 number: they believe the testimony of others. Hebrews 11 is like that. This "Faith Hall of Fame" tells the stories of people in the Bible who endured hardship and kept going. They kept the faith. This chapter is in the Bible to inspire us spiritually.

Today, spend some time being inspired. Find something to fuel your "this can be done" muscle. That is a good thing to do throughout the process of pursuing your dreams, but I want you to really focus on it today.

1. Ask God to lead you to some inspiration in the Bible as well as in other places. Read the passages about faith that always speak to you. Turn to Psalm 37:4 ("Delight

yourself in the LORD and he will give you the desires of your heart") or Proverbs 3:5–6 ("Trust in the LORD with all your heart and lean not on your own understanding; in all your ways acknowledge him, and he will make your paths straight"). Read an inspirational book. Google your topic for testimonies from those who have achieved your dream.

2. Talk to someone who has accomplished what you are trying to do and ask them to tell you their story again.

DAY 28

Notice Your Triggers

Everyone has things that trip them up. For some people, those things are stress, discouragement, or failure. For others, as we have seen, difficult people can trip them up. For still others, it is the fact that pursuing a dream takes time. Some folks are sidetracked by people infringing on their dedicated work time. You looked at your past patterns on Day 20 and noticed the ways and reasons you have failed in the past. Now it's time to identify those ways you're struggling in *this* process—and then go one step further: identify the triggers.

Triggers are the things that begin the process of your going downhill. They are the things that set you off, and from there the pattern kicks in. For example, I know an addict who does well on his goal of sobriety until he has a difficult interaction with any authority figure. If his boss is not pleased with him, that is the moment he begins a slide toward discouragement that can land him in the gutter. For years, that trigger would get to him—until he identified it.

Once he did, this man was ready for it. Whenever he had to talk to his boss, he would first call his sponsor and get ready; he would also call his sponsor afterward. If he was discouraged, he would know to go to an AA meeting. He had defeated the power of that trigger in his life.

You have been working toward your goal for a while now, and I want you to see what little triggers may be derailing—or trying to derail—your efforts to accomplish your dream.

1. As you look at this current process, do you notice familiar patterns kicking in? If so, what are the triggers that prompt them?

2. If the old patterns are not kicking in, are new patterns of discouragement and failure arising? What are the triggers that prompt those? What can you do to avoid those triggers? Be specific.

3. What help do you need to avoid those triggers? Who can help?

DAY 29

Assess Your Progress and Plan for the Future

You are almost at the end of the thirty days. All along the way, I have asked you to take gut checks, make time for reality checks, look at your patterns, etc. In other words, self-observation has been an important part of this program, as it always is in achieving goals. Now it's time to go a step further: it's time to figure out where exactly you are and what you are going to do from here.

As we said in the beginning, thirty days is not enough to accomplish big dreams. But it is enough time to get you started down the right path. So today I want you to think about where you are going to go from here.

I. Where are you now? What dream have you fulfilled or made progress on? Some dreams—like facing a difficult relationship or cleaning up a garage that has been sitting there messy for ten years—can be accomplished in a short time. Other dreams are long-term, so the better questions are "Where are you in the process? Have you gotten a good beginning? Have you stalled out somewhere? What steps, if any, do you need to go back and focus on for a while?" So where are you now? Talk either about a short-term dream that you've accomplished or about progress you've made toward realizing a long-term dream.

2. As you move forward, go back through this thirty-day plan and look at the steps that you need to repeat. Know that it is OK to repeat steps. In fact, that is normal for success. Also realize that people make a critical time path (Day 12) and then readjust and fine-tune it as an ongoing part of their efforts to achieve their goal. You may need to repeat some of the inner work or camp out on some other steps, like identifying and overcoming patterns of defeat.

3. Move now from thinking about and pursuing the beginning, short-term program to developing a longer-range plan of how you are going to use the next year to keep moving toward fulfilling your dream. Which steps have you completed? Which steps do you need to commit to continue on an ongoing basis?

4. Now plan your next thirty days using some of the steps you have covered, and then take a stab at planning the next six months or a year.

5. You may want to include some of the individual steps from your first thirty days in the next plan. For a period of time, for example, you may want to keep working on dealing with difficult people. You may have learned that you need to camp out there for a few months to get that taken care of in a deeper way.

6. Write all your thoughts down into a plan and share it with your group, counselor, or accountability partner. Then decide how you are going to keep the structure that this program has provided you.

DAY 30

Recommit for the Future

In Matthew 6:33 Jesus says to "seek first his kingdom and his righteousness, and all these things will be given to you as well." The "all these things" mentioned there are the things that all of us seek: our concerns, dreams, and goals as well as our everyday needs. The Bible says that we are made to put God first, and when we do, the rest will follow. That is why we began this program by seeing God accurately, because he is the source of life and of your dreams.

Romans 12 begins with a similar idea. Here are the first two verses:

> Therefore, I urge you, brothers, in view of God's mercy, to offer your bodies as living sacrifices, holy and pleasing to God—this is your spiritual act of worship. Do not conform any longer to the pattern of this world, but be transformed by the renewing of your mind. *Then you will be able to test and approve what God's will is—his good, pleasing and perfect will.*
>
> (emphasis added)

The idea that God is to be the source of your life and of your dreams and goals is clear throughout the Bible. He will provide, guide, empower, preserve, and celebrate with you. Your job is to respond to his call for a relationship with you, to accept his invitation to abide in him, and to step out in faith and develop your talents to the best of your ability.

So, as I leave you to continue pursuing your dream from here, I want to remind you to continue with God, the Source of it all.

1. What have you learned about God in the last thirty days? Where have you seen him show up in your life and specifically in your pursuit of your dream? Be specific.

2. What have you learned about your commitment to God in the last thirty days? Since starting to fulfill your dreams, have you gone to him more than ever, less than before, or about the same as usual? What could you do to improve in your faithfulness to God?

3. What in the last thirty days would you like to thank God for? What would you like to celebrate with him? God *loves* a good party, so jump up and down right where you are and celebrate what you have accomplished or learned.

4. If you are discouraged, know that is part of the process. Discouragement helps you figure out where your roadblocks are or realize that you need more help. Ask God to help you find the kind of help you need—and then go get it! If you haven't accomplished what you had wanted to by this time, just let that be a diagnosis that God has allowed you to see that you need help. That can actually be his message—and an important lesson—to you from the last thirty days.

5. Plan a structure for your spiritual life on an ongoing basis. You need good individual time with God as well as a good church, a good group, and a smaller circle of friends with whom you do your spiritual life, like sharing, encouraging, and praying together. Which of these aspects of your spiritual life are already in place? What steps will you take to develop those that aren't in place or to strengthen those that are weak? Who will your ongoing community and team be?

6. Include in your plan a list of resources and places of learning. Write down the names of books, retreats, Web sites, CDs, etc. Go visit my Web site www.solutionsonvideo.com for some good growth material.

Prayer

God, thank you for the last thirty days, for my victories, and for my defeats. Thank you for what I have learned. Help me to use it to continue along the path with you. Show me my next steps and provide the resources that I need to continue to reach the Promised Land that you have helped me define. Amen.